How To Cope With OCD

Practical Strategies on How to Deal With OCD

John Annabel

Table of Contents

Chapter 1

Understanding OCD

On occasion, it is normal to go back and double-check that the Electric Cooker is unplugged, to be concerned that you have been contaminated by germs, or to have an unpleasant, violent thought. However, if you have obsessive-compulsive disorder (OCD), obsessive thoughts and compulsive behaviors can become so overwhelming that they interfere with your daily life.

OCD is defined by uncontrollable, unwanted thoughts and ritualized, repetitive behaviors that you feel compelled to engage in. If you have OCD, you are probably aware that your obsessive thoughts and compulsive behaviors are irrational, but you are still unable to resist them and break free.

Like a needle stuck on an old record, OCD causes the brain to become fixated on a specific thought or urge. For example, you may check the stove 30 times to ensure that it is truly turned off because you are afraid of burning down your house, or you may scrub your hands raw out of fear of germs. While performing these repetitive behaviors does not bring you pleasure, they may provide some temporary relief from the anxiety caused by obsessive thoughts.

You may try to avoid situations that cause or exacerbate your symptoms, or you may use alcohol or drugs to self-medicate. While it may appear that you can't escape your obsessions and compulsions, there are numerous things you can do to break free from unwanted thoughts and irrational urges and regain control of your thoughts and actions.

Historically, OCD was classified as an anxiety disorder under the Diagnostic and Statistical Manual of Mental Disorders (DSM). Nevertheless, OCD was moved out of the "Anxiety Disorders" section of the DSM in the fifth edition, and a new section named "Obsessive-Compulsive and Related Conditions" was added.

The change was made after researchers discovered significant differences between OCD and anxiety disorders. For example, with OCD, you respond to unwanted thoughts with repetitive, ineffective rituals. You may or may not be aware that your thoughts and compulsions, such as frequent hand washing, are irrational. However, anxiety causes you to ruminate on real-world concerns, such as a fear of being mocked or judged. You may respond by avoiding the source of your fear, but you will not use strange rituals to relieve your distress.

Certain treatments for OCD and anxiety disorders may also differ. To deal with an anxiety disorder, you may need to gradually confront your fears, whereas treating OCD requires addressing the compulsive behavior.

Obsessions are involuntary thoughts, images, or impulses that repeat in your mind. You don't want to have these thoughts, but you can't avoid them. Unfortunately, these obsessive thoughts are frequently disruptive and distracting.

Compulsions are behaviors or rituals that you feel compelled to repeat over and over. Compulsions are typically used to relieve obsessions. For example, if you're concerned about contamination, you might develop elaborate cleaning rituals. However, the relief does not last. In fact, obsessive thoughts often return stronger. Compulsive rituals and behaviors frequently cause anxiety as they become more demanding and time-consuming, this is a vicious cycle of OCD.

Hoarding & OCD

Hoarding was previously classified as an OCD disorder. While estimates suggest that up to 25% of people with OCD engage in compulsive hoarding, it can also be a symptom of a separate condition, hoarding disorder.

Hoarders are afraid that throwing anything away will result in something bad, so they keep things they don't need or use. However, there is a difference between OCD-related hoarding and hoarding disorder.

OCD-related hoarders do not collect so many possessions that their homes become unmanageable. Hoarding is typically unwelcome and distressing for them, serving as a means of coping with intrusive thoughts.

In contrast, someone with hoarding disorder experiences both positive and negative emotions. Acquiring possessions brings pleasure rather than simply satisfying a compulsion, and being surrounded by their belongings provides comfort. The distress in hoarding disorder is caused more by the consequences of hoarding—clutter and an unsafe environment—as well as the anxiety of having to discard possessions.

The Four Categories of OCD

Obsessions and compulsions can involve a wide range of topics. However, the majority of them fall into four categories. You can have obsessive thoughts and compulsions that fit into multiple categories. You may have obsessions and compulsions that differ from those listed below.

Unacceptable or taboo thoughts

Persons with this type of OCD have intrusive thoughts that are inappropriate for their values, whether sexual, violent, or taboo. Everyone may have an "unacceptable" thought on occasion. However, people with OCD may have a harder time letting these thoughts go. "Taboo" thoughts frequently revolve around a few major themes, such as:

Sexual orientation OCD
These intrusive thoughts/obsessions center on the individual's sexual orientation. They may frequently question their sexual attraction to others. And they may seek reassurance from others about their sexual orientation on a regular basis.

Relationship OCD
It is not uncommon to have moments of doubt in a relationship. But relationship OCD extends beyond these common concerns. It may cause a person to constantly question whether they are in a relationship with the "right" person. They may also become fixated on their partner's "flaws" and character traits.

OCD causes harm
Someone with OCD is concerned about their ability or willingness to harm others. They may injure themselves, their loved ones, or even a stranger as a result of this fear. It could be accompanied by disturbing violent images or thoughts.

Pedophilia OCD
These intrusive thoughts/obsessions stem from fears of being sexually attracted to or harming children. Even if there is no evidence to back up this suspicion, the individual may have distressing doubts about being a pedophile.

Scrupulosity OCD

A person with OCD that fits this theme may constantly monitor themselves for "immoral" or "sinful" behavior, thoughts, or feelings. Their intrusive thoughts and obsessions are about moral, ethical, or religious issues.

People with taboo obsessions may exhibit less obvious compulsions. They frequently engage in other types of compulsions to alleviate their anxiety, including:

> ➤ *Thought suppression or intentionally trying not to have a thought.*
> ➤ *Seeking assurance from others.*
> ➤ *Obsessively praying*

These thoughts are especially upsetting because they do not reflect the person's values. In general, someone with OCD will avoid committing the acts they fear. Instead, they may go to great lengths to avoid having these thoughts.

Doubt and Double-Checking

People with OCD frequently lack trust in their own memory and judgment. Doubt is a key component of all types of OCD. However, some people have a particularly difficult time doubting their own perception of reality. They may also doubt their ability to recall recent events.

A person with this type of OCD may leave the house, lock their door, and then wonder if they actually locked their door when they get into their car. This could be a common experience for many people. However, someone with OCD may need to check back several times before trusting that the task is complete.

Another characteristic of OCD is incompleteness or the feeling that something is not "just right". For example, someone with OCD may lock their door repeatedly. Even if the door was properly locked the first time, this sense of incompleteness can drive them to repeat the task until it feels "just right."

Contamination and washing

People with this type of OCD have obsessive thoughts about becoming ill and spreading germs. Their compulsions are related to cleanliness but go far beyond the typical ways people practice hygiene and cleaning. For instance, someone with contamination OCD might:

➢ *Create rituals that include repeatedly washing their hands until they bleed.*
➢ *Excessive usage of bleach and other cleaning products to ensure their environment is free of contaminants.*
➢ *Refrain from touching everyday objects like door knobs and using public restrooms.*

According to research, people who develop this type of OCD may experience oversensitive disgust reactions. This means they experience disgust more frequently than the average person. They then struggle to let go of the emotion. Aside from dirt and germs, people with contamination OCD may develop fears of:

➢ *Blood*
➢ *spoiled food*
➢ *Bodily Fluids*
➢ *Broken glass*

Ordering and Arranging

People with this type of OCD may become fixated on order and symmetry in their surroundings. This is not the same as enjoying keeping your home organized. People with this type of OCD can spend hours of their day rearranging the same objects until they meet a specific standard. Examples of compulsions in this category include:

➢ *Reorganizing items in your home until they feel "right"*
➢ *Moving items a specific number of times, such as putting the same book on a shelf eight times, because that number has special meaning.*
➢ *Counting items repeatedly.*

The most common forms of OCD are contamination and germ OCD. This type of OCD affects up to 46% of people who have received an OCD diagnosis.

Unfortunately, attempting to avoid thinking about something usually produces the opposite effect. Avoiding an intrusive thought makes it more likely to return.

Chapter 2

The Effects of OCD on Daily Life

People with Obsessive-Compulsive Disorder are in a constant state of distress due to intrusive thoughts and accompanying compulsions aimed at reducing anxiety, which ultimately affects their quality of life. Obsessions and compulsions can have a significant impact on one's quality of life, making even basic tasks difficult. Here are some of the ways that OCD can affect different aspects of your life:

Personal and Social Relationships
One of the most difficult aspects of living with OCD is its effect on personal and social relationships. Individuals with OCD may struggle to engage in social activities or maintain relationships due to the time-consuming nature of compulsions. Fear of being judged or misunderstood by others can also lead to isolation and loneliness.

Furthermore, OCD can put a strain on family relationships. It can be difficult for family members to understand the individual's compulsive behavior and inability to control their obsessions. This lack of understanding can cause tension, conflict, and emotional distress within the family.

Performance
OCD has a significant impact on educational and occupational performance. Students with OCD may struggle to focus on their studies due to recurring obsessions. They may also spend a significant amount of time performing rituals, which impedes their academic progress.

Similarly, people with OCD may have difficulty being productive at work. They may struggle to meet deadlines or complete tasks efficiently because of the time spent on compulsions. Obsession-related anxiety can also make it difficult to focus, resulting in poor performance.

Overwhelming doubts
Individuals with Obsessive-Compulsive Disorder have difficulty concentrating due to intense doubt. Compulsions are frequently used to alleviate these doubts; for example, a cleanliness obsession may lead to excessive handwashing.

Interference with Daily Life

Perfectionism is a common trait in OCD patients, making even simple tasks difficult due to a lack of concentration and unrealistic expectations. Obsessive-Compulsive Disorder disrupts everyday life by causing anxiety and interfering with routine tasks.

Disturbance in relationships

OCD can strain relationships because people demand specific behaviors from loved ones and are constantly concerned about their well-being. Family members who understand the nature of OCD are better able to offer support. Education about the disorder helps to dispel myths and foster empathy.

Self-Harm

Ritualistic compulsions to relieve anxiety can lead to self-harm, such as picking at hair or skin during intrusive thoughts. Excessive hand washing can also cause skin issues.

Consuming Drugs

Some people may use drugs or engage in other activities to cope with persistent negative thoughts and the desire to perform actions to alleviate anxiety caused by repetitive thought patterns.

Physical Health

OCD is primarily a mental health disorder, but it can also have a physical impact. Chronic stress and anxiety from OCD can cause a variety of physical health problems, including headaches, gastrointestinal issues, and fatigue. Furthermore, compulsive behaviors like excessive washing can cause physical harm, such as skin irritation or injury.

Emotional Wellbeing

Finally, and perhaps most importantly, OCD has a significant impact on emotional well-being. Constantly wrestling with intrusive thoughts can be extremely distressing, resulting in feelings of frustration, guilt, and despair. OCD's chronic nature, combined with the difficulty of managing symptoms, can lead to the development of other mental health disorders such as depression or anxiety disorders.

Common myths about OCD coping skills

There are a few common myths about OCD coping skills that can be misleading and prevent people from effectively managing their condition.

Here, we address some of these misconceptions by providing clear and accurate information.

OCD coping skills can cure OCD entirely

While OCD coping skills are important for managing symptoms and improving quality of life, they are not a cure for OCD. The goal is to help people live with their condition more comfortably and without being too disrupted by their symptoms.

OCD coping skills are identical to ordinary stress management techniques

While some OCD coping strategies may overlap with general stress management techniques, they are distinct. OCD coping skills are designed to address the unique challenges of OCD, such as intrusive thoughts and compulsive actions.

OCD coping skills are only effective in therapy

While therapy can offer a structured and guided environment for learning and practicing OCD coping skills, these abilities can also be used independently. They are designed to be practical tools that people with OCD can use to manage their symptoms at any time and from any location.

OCD coping skills are simply about suppressing obsessive thoughts

Contrary to popular belief, many OCD coping strategies involve acknowledging and accepting thoughts, rather than suppressing them. Mindfulness and cognitive reframing techniques, for example, aim to change the relationship with obsessive thoughts rather than eliminate them.

Seeking Professional Diagnosis and Assessment.

It is important to understand that there is no single type of OCD assessment. Different types of assessments may be more or less appropriate based on the individual's needs and circumstances. There are primarily four types of OCD assessments, which include:

Clinical Interview

A structured clinical interview is a common method of assessing OCD. This is usually done with a mental health professional, which includes a psychiatrist, psychologist, or clinical social worker. It entails asking inquiries regarding your symptoms, thoughts, and actions.

Furthermore, this type helps to rule out any other mental health disorders that could be causing your symptoms. The interviewer will ask questions about the individual with OCD. They will also inquire about other aspects of functioning, such as employment and relationships. Eventually, during these interviews, a mental health professional will issue a diagnosis.

Self-report measures
Self-report measures are another way to assess OCD. This can take the form of a paper and pencil questionnaire or an online survey. It usually asks about your symptoms and how they have affected your life. Self-report measures are commonly used to screen for OCD and monitor symptoms over time. They can also be used to determine the severity of OCD symptoms, which is referred to as a psychological evaluation.

Observational measures
Observational measures are another way to assess OCD. This usually entails observing the person with OCD in various situations, such as during a conversation or while performing a task. More often, this involves observing the person perform difficult activities or tasks, such as cleaning or organizing. The clinician can then look for any patterns or issues that may exist.

The observer will keep track of any unusual behaviors or mannerisms. They may also inquire about the individual's thoughts and feelings regarding their obsessive-compulsive behaviors. Observational measures can help assess the severity of OCD symptoms and how they affect the person's life.

Medical examination
A medical examination can rule out any physical causes of your symptoms. This is especially important if you have new-onset OCD. A healthcare provider will take a medical history and order tests to rule out any underlying physical conditions.

Physical examination tests are important because some medical conditions can cause symptoms similar to OCD. For example, an overactive thyroid gland may trigger anxiety and obsessive thoughts. Once any physical causes of your symptoms have been eliminated, you can focus on treating your OCD.

These are the most common ways to assess OCD. A mental health professional can conduct an OCD assessment and devise a treatment plan. With the right treatment, many people with OCD can live healthy and productive lives.

The Benefits of OCD Assessment

There are numerous advantages to receiving an OCD assessment. It can help people:

> ➤ ***Know more about their condition.***
> ➤ ***Gain a better understanding of their symptoms***
> ➤ ***Discover what OCD treatment options are available to them.***
> ➤ ***Start the process of recovering from OCD.***

An OCD assessment can also help family members and friends of someone with OCD. It can help them understand the disorder and how best to support their loved ones during treatment.

Furthermore, it is critical to remember that an OCD assessment is the first step toward treatment. It is not a diagnostic tool, but rather a method for beginning to understand and address OCD symptoms. Contact a psychologist or psychiatrist to begin the OCD assessment process.

However, this is not a quick or simple test. The assessment takes time to complete. If you're ready to take the first step in your OCD recovery journey, you must answer each question as honestly as possible to ensure the most accurate results.

Chapter 3

Root Causes of OCD

Although OCD affects a large number of people, its underlying causes are not fully understood. On the other hand, a mix of environment, brain chemistry, and heredity is thought to be responsible. Here are some factors that have been linked to OCD and may aggravate or increase the risk of symptoms in those who are susceptible to the disorder:

Upbringing

Helicopter parents are more likely to be overprotective, which may increase some children's vulnerability to OCD. Other potential risk factors for developing OCD include having a lot of responsibility as a child or being subjected to extremely strict rules. Stressful or distressing situations can trigger or worsen symptoms in people who are predisposed to OCD.

It is still too early to draw definitive conclusions about these links and how genes may interact with childhood experiences to increase the risk of developing OCD. We know a lot about addressing OCD once it's diagnosed, but little about how and when it develops.

Sleep habits and patterns

Yes, lack of sleep exacerbates all symptoms, including OCD. Your bedtime and sleep duration predict your ability to control or resist obsessive thoughts. In a 2018 study published in Sleep, individuals with OCD who went to bed after midnight had a more difficult time controlling obsessive thoughts. Furthermore, a 2018 study published in the Journal of Behavior Therapy and Experimental Psychiatry found that people who sleep less than the recommended eight hours per night are more likely to experience intrusive, repetitive thoughts. Light box therapy may help to reset circadian rhythms and improve the quality and quantity of sleep. The research is ongoing, but sitting in front of a light box for 30 minutes per day can help move the sleep cycle forward and reduce OCD symptoms. Lightboxes are generally safe, but they should not be used by people who have specific eye problems or are sensitive to sunlight.

Brain inflammation

Scientists may have discovered one potential factor contributing to OCD inflammation. According to a 2017 study published in JAMA Psychiatry, brain scans of people with OCD revealed that inflammation was 32% higher in six brain regions known to play a role in OCD than in those without OCD. Furthermore, previous research in the Journal of Neuroinflammation indicates that brain inflammation may play a role in other psychiatric conditions such as major depressive disorder, schizophrenia, and bipolar disorder. If researchers can find a way to reduce the negative side effects of inflammation, it could help in the development of treatments for these conditions.

Fear of Losing Control

People with OCD may feel compelled to double-check things like turning off the stove and locking the door. According to research, a fear of losing control may be linked to the checking behaviors that characterize OCD. In a 2017 study published in the Journal of Obsessive-Compulsive and Related Disorders, psychology researchers looked at 130+ college students and told some, but not others, that they were at greater chance of losing control over their ideas and actions based on "EEG evidence." In a lab experiment where participants had to regulate the speed of images, those who believed they were at higher risk of losing control were twice as likely to double-check which keys to use as those who did not believe they were at risk of losing control. The researchers hypothesized that people's fear and beliefs about losing control could put them at risk for a variety of psychiatric disorders, including OCD, generalized anxiety disorder, and panic disorder, among others.

Your exposure to specific types of bacteria

Pediatric autoimmune neuropsychiatric disorders associated with streptococcal infections (PANDAS) refer to the rare, sudden, and dramatic onset of OCD and/or tic disorders following a strep infection, or the worsening of such after a strep infection. According to the International OCD Foundation, PANDAS most commonly affects children aged 4 to 14 years. It occurs when the immune system misfires in response to a strep infection and attacks the brain. According to the National Institute of Mental Health, treating strep with antibiotics is the most effective way to combat PANDAS. While they will gradually fade after treatment, symptoms may reappear if strep returns. Because PANDAS is so uncommon, many other possibilities must be considered before a diagnosis is made.

Your stress or pent-up anger

No, anger does not cause OCD. However, when someone with OCD internalizes anger and rage, their symptoms may worsen. "Internalized anger, if not expressed, such as through communication, exercise, or another outlet, must go somewhere, often leading to depression, anxiety, and OCD. OCD flares are not uncommon during stressful or angry times. Seeking treatment is critical as researchers attempt to identify the cause of OCD. OCD can be severely debilitating, but there are treatments available. Cognitive behavior therapy, talk therapy, and medications can all be effective in treating OCD.

Your fear of guilt
According to a 2017 study published in the journal Clinical Psychology & Psychotherapy, OCD may be influenced by an intense fear of guilt. The researchers discovered that people with OCD may perceive guilt as more threatening than others, making it intolerable for them. Any thought or impulse that evokes guilt may be met with intense anxiety and compulsive behavior. Importantly, this applies to being extremely sensitive to guilt, not just being guilt-prone.

Your birth circumstances
According to a 2016 study published in JAMA Psychiatry, people who were born via C-section, preterm or breech, were unusually large or small as babies or had a mother who smoked 10 cigarettes or more per day during pregnancy appear to be at a higher risk of developing OCD. In a study of 2.4 million children in Sweden, approximately 17,000 developed OCD, with an average age at diagnosis of 23.

The researchers discovered that the more of these individual elements an infant encountered, the higher the risk of developing OCD. However, this type of study cannot prove that those factors caused the OCD; it can only show that they were associated with it. The study is yet another reason to encourage women to quit smoking while pregnant.

Chapter 4

Treatment Options

Because this behavior exacerbates rather than relieves the individual's anxiety, the obsessive thoughts and compulsive actions that define OCD amplify one another, necessitating treatment that can provide OCD symptom relief. There are currently several established OCD treatment options, each with varying levels of efficacy and potential side effects. It is recommended that you consult with your doctor to determine the best treatment for your specific symptoms and needs.

Deep TMS
Deep Transcranial Magnetic Stimulation is a novel treatment method that employs magnetic fields to safely, effectively, and non-invasively reach brain structures related to mental health conditions.

Deep TMS has been FDA-cleared to treat OCD since 2018, demonstrating its ability to provide significant relief to those suffering from this condition. This observation was confirmed by a 2019 multicenter, sham-controlled clinical research study published in the American Journal of Psychiatry, which found Deep TMS to effectively and safely alleviate OCD symptoms, even among patients who had not improved sufficiently with medication or therapy.

Deep TMS is a non-invasive form of therapy that does not require anesthesia, can be integrated into an individual's daily routine, and has no long-term or significant side effects.

Cognitive behavior therapy (CBT)
CBT is a type of talk therapy that is used as a first-line treatment for OCD. CBT, when administered by a trained mental health professional, focuses on the thoughts, feelings, behaviors, and physical reactions associated with OCD. This is done to familiarize the patient with the condition's various facets and gradually alleviate its symptoms.

Several types of therapy have evolved from CBT over time to provide patients with OCD with greater symptom relief. Acceptance and commitment therapy (ACT) is the most notable of these: ACT encourages openness and flexibility in response to OCD symptoms, as the therapist assists the patient in defining and carrying out a commitment to their own well-being.

Exposure and Response Therapy (ERP)

ERP is a form of therapy that has been shown to effectively treat OCD. ERP assists the patient in overcoming OCD by gradually exposing them to stimuli associated with OCD-inducing anxiety. The patient is encouraged to avoid reacting to stimuli in a forced manner, and they gradually become accustomed to managing OCD-related, anxiety-inducing behavior.

Psychopharmacology

Medication is another type of therapy that is frequently used as the first line of treatment for OCD. The FDA has approved several selective serotonin reuptake inhibitors (SSRIs), including the branded medications Prozac and Zoloft, as well as one tricyclic antidepressant (TCA), to treat the condition, with SSRIs being among the most frequently prescribed class of medication.

Though many patients suffering from OCD symptoms report relief from psychopharmacology, many also experience a variety of side effects and may decide to discontinue this form of treatment due to their severity.

Psychodynamic therapy has also been shown to help patients with OCD. This treatment focuses on the relationships and events that, among other aspects of the patient's life, are fundamental to their sense of self, worldview, and personal narrative. These elements are then examined in relation to the negative OCD symptoms they are experiencing, in order to gain a better understanding of the underlying reasons for how they respond to the anxiety their condition causes. Over time, the patient should be able to transition away from automatically responding to induced anxiety and toward more flexible, calming, and beneficial reactions.

Other Invasive Treatments

Despite the various options available to those suffering from OCD, some patients do not find relief from first-line or non-invasive OCD treatments. As a result, healthcare professionals may offer neurosurgical options to treatment-resistant patients.

Recent studies using various neurological lesion methods have shown some efficacy in reducing OCD symptoms in treatment-resistant patients. Gamma knife coagulative lesions, radioactive seed implants that cause local ablations, and standard craniotomy are among the methods used. Ablative neurosurgical options always focus on the brain's cortico-striato-thalamo-cortical circuit, which is thought to become hyperactive in patients with OCD.

In addition to the invasiveness and recovery time required after such procedures, it should be noted that studies examining these techniques are typically based on open trials with a small number of patients. As a result, their efficacy in the general OCD population has yet to be established, necessitating larger, blinded studies to determine how effective they are in reducing OCD symptoms.

Tips for a Successful OCD Treatment

Here, he lists some tips for successful OCD treatment:

OCD can sometimes make you doubt your homework.
It may indicate that you are not receiving appropriate treatment, that your assignments cannot possibly improve you, or that you simply do not understand what you are doing and will not be able to make it work. Remember that OCD is known as the Doubting Disease, and it will attempt to cast doubt on anything important to you. To combat this, you may have to agree with it, saying, "Yes, that's correct. "I really won't get better."

Never forget you have OCD
This means you won't always be able to trust your own reactions or what you think and feel, especially if they appear to be telling you something negative and extreme. If you're unsure whether something is a symptom, treat it as such. It's better to get a little more exposure than not enough.

Remember that the problem with OCD is not anxiety, but compulsions
If you believe that anxiety is the problem, you will engage in more compulsions to overcome it. If you recognize that the compulsions are the problem, stop engaging in them, and remain in the fearful situation, the anxiety will eventually subside as you develop tolerance.

Always expect the unexpected
Obsessive thoughts can occur at any time or in any location. Don't be surprised if old or new ones appear. Don't let it bother you. Be prepared to use your therapy tools at any time and from any location. Also, if new thoughts arise, notify your therapist so that they can stay informed.

Be willing to take risks
Risk is an unavoidable part of life, and thus cannot be completely eliminated. Remember that not recovering is the greatest risk of all.

Never seek reassurance from yourself or others
Instead, tell yourself that the worst will happen, is happening, or has already occurred. Reassurance will negate the effects of any therapy homework you complete and prevent you from progressing. Reassurance-seeking is a compulsion, regardless of how you justify it.

Always strive to agree with all obsessive thoughts
Never analyze, question, or argue with them. The questions they pose are not real, and there are no real answers to them. When agreeing, try not to go into too much detail; simply state that the thoughts are true and real.

Don't waste time trying to stop or avoid thinking your thoughts
This will only have the opposite effect, leading to more thoughts. Studies have shown that you cannot effectively stop or suppress specific thoughts. "If you want to think regarding them less, think about them more."

Try not to think in black-and-white, all-or-nothing terms
Don't tell yourself that one slip-up means you're a complete failure. If you slip and engage in a compulsion, you can always reverse it and do something to cancel it. The good news is that you're in it for the long haul, and you'll always have another chance. It is normal to make mistakes when learning new skills, particularly in therapy. It happens to everyone now and again. Accept it. Even if you experience a major setback, don't let it derail you.

Remember the saying: 'A lapse is not actually a relapse, which implies that you can never truly start over. To do so, you would have to forget everything you had learned up to that point, which is simply not possible. Keep in mind the mantras, "You can always start over," and "Never confuse a single defeat with a final defeat," as they say in AA.

Remember that you are solely responsible for dealing with your symptoms
Do not include others in your therapy homework (unless your therapist instructs you to) or expect them to push or motivate you. They won't always be available when you need them, but you will always be there for yourself.

Don't become impatient with your progress or compare yourself to others
Everyone moves at their own pace. Instead, try to focus on completing each day's therapy homework, one at a time.

When given the option, always choose to face your anxiety rather than avoid it
The only way to overcome fear (anxiety) is to confront it. You can't get away from your own thoughts, so you have no choice but to confront them. If you want to recover, you must do this.

If your therapist assigns you an assignment that you do not feel prepared to complete, you can speak up and let them know.
As a member of the therapist-patient team, you should have a say in your own treatment. The goal is for the homework to cause you some anxiety so that you can get used to tolerating it, rather than to overwhelm you and set you back. On the other hand, don't be afraid to challenge yourself whenever possible.

Do not wait for the "perfect moment" to begin your therapy homework assignments
Many people with OCD suffer from procrastination, so begin working on your therapy homework assignments as soon as you receive them. The ideal time is whenever you start doing them.

Don't get sidetracked by perfectionism
OCD can also include perfectionism. Your OCD may tell you that if you don't complete your homework perfectly, you won't recover. If you find yourself obsessing over having to do your homework perfectly, you risk developing another compulsion.

Keep an eye out for homework assignments that require you to follow the same rigid rules every time. Also, don't do so much homework that it takes up the entire day, remember, you still have a life to live.

Try to review your homework assignments at the beginning of each day
Don't assume you know them all and will never forget them.

When completing assignments, be careful not to reassure yourself and undo your hard work

It can be detrimental to all of the hard work you have done to tell yourself things like, "It's only a home assignment, and the things I'm actually doing don't count and aren't real," or, "My therapist wouldn't ask me to do a thing that would cause harm to me or those around them," or, "I'm only doing these things because I did as instructed, so I can't hold myself accountable for any negative outcomes."

Give your homework your complete attention, concentrate on what you're doing, and allow yourself to feel the anxiety
Try not to tune out while working on certain assignments so that you don't feel anxious. People sometimes let homework become routine and do it in an automatic manner as a form of avoidance. Also, do not do homework while engaging in other distracting activities. You are developing tolerance for what you fear, which requires you to be present with it.

When confronted with a difficult assignment or an unexpectedly difficult situation, try to view it positively
Instead of saying, "Oh, no. "Why do I have to do this?" Instead, tell yourself, "This will be good for me, another opportunity to practice and get stronger. Try not to rush through your therapy homework so that you can feel less anxious.

Take your time and consider all of the benefits it will bring you. The goal is not to get through it as quickly as possible; rather, it is to raise a moderate level of anxiety and persevere.

If your homework does not cause you any anxiety, tell your therapist about it
If your exposure to homework does not cause some level of anxiety, it will not be very beneficial to you. On the other hand, give all new assignments at least a week before deciding they don't make you nervous. Some assignments can elicit reactions later on, and it may take a few attempts before anxiety develops.

Always remember to be proud of your own efforts and celebrate your successes
It's a good way to maintain your motivation. If you believe you are not making progress, review previous assignments that are no longer challenging.

Never forget that OCD is extremely paradoxical and rarely makes sense
The things you thought would make you improve only make you worse, and the things you believed would make you worse will actually make you better.

Chapter 5

Mindfulness Practices for OCD

Mindfulness is an innate ability that all humans possess but may not understand how to use. Mindfulness is fundamentally about being fully present and aware. This means that when you practice mindfulness, you understand that the thoughts that arise in your mind are not what defines you, and you are not obligated to act on them. When you practice intentional mindfulness, you experience your thoughts as an observer, processing them more deeply and critically.

You can also feel or experience your breath and body, which allows your mind to relax and process its surroundings. This can help many individuals feel less overwhelmed or reactive, and it may particularly assist those with OCD in processing their thoughts about their compulsions and avoiding acting on them.

A 2013 study comparing the use of mindfulness and meditation to the use of distraction in 30 OCD patients found that those who used mindfulness skills felt less compelled to give in to their compulsions, whereas those who used distraction techniques saw no change.

When you have OCD, mindfulness can be especially difficult because being in the present moment can involve stressful intrusive thoughts, feelings, and sensations. When you practice mindfulness, you are asked to intentionally allow these intrusive thoughts or feelings to exist rather than attempting to stop them through compulsion. In this sense, mindfulness is similar to exposure and response prevention (ERP).

ERP encourages OCD sufferers to confront their triggers and fight the urge to neutralize them with compulsions. Mindfulness requires you to be conscious of intrusive thoughts or triggers, accept and possibly internalize any discomforts caused by such thoughts, and resist the urge to respond with compulsions. Both practices involve taking a deeper and longer look at your initial reactions or thoughts and working to avoid responding to them. This action in mindfulness shifts your brain out of fight-or-flight mode, giving you the time and space to fully process, relax, and gain control over your compulsions.

Ways to Practice Mindfulness

There are many free resources available to help you begin with mindfulness techniques. Different techniques often work for different people; there is no right or wrong way to practice mindfulness, and it is often necessary to experiment to determine which method is best for you. Some mindfulness techniques are:

> ➤ *Purposeful breaks are taken throughout the day.*
> ➤ *Meditations that occur while sitting, walking, or moving.*
> ➤ *Meditation combined with physical activity, such as practicing yoga or sports.*

Meditation can be especially effective for mindfulness because it requires you to connect with your breath and body, which often naturally draws you out of intrusive or cyclical thoughts. When you're focused on sitting in the proper posture and breathing deeply, your mind can be distracted from wandering and brought back to your connection with the body.

Where to Practice Mindfulness

The benefit of practicing mindfulness is that it can be used whenever and wherever you are. If you notice intrusive thoughts creeping in, take a moment to sit with them and breathe. Allow the thoughts to be, and resist the urge to respond to any compulsions they may elicit. You can practice this while sitting in public, meditating alone in your bedroom, or at the grocery store filling your cart. It simply requires a moment of stillness or the ability to pause and observe your thoughts.

The most common misconception about mindfulness is that it requires you to sit and meditate silently. This is not the case, as there are numerous techniques for incorporating mindfulness into your daily life! You could practice mindfulness while running on the treadmill or listening to your favorite album. It's all about taking the time to fully experience the present moment, no matter where you are.

Getting Started with Mindfulness

One option is to meditate. A basic method is to concentrate your attention on your own breathing, a practice commonly referred to as "mindful breathing. After dedicating time to mindful breathing, you'll find it easier to focus attention on your breath in everyday life, which is an important skill for dealing with stress, anxiety, and negative emotions, cooling down when your temper flares, and sharpening your ability to concentrate.

15 minutes per day for at least a week, though research suggests that mindfulness improves with practice.

The most basic method of mindful breathing is to concentrate your attention on your breath, both inhaling and exhaling. You can do this standing, but it's best to sit or lie down in a comfortable position. Your eyes can be open or closed, but closing them may help you focus more effectively. It can help to schedule this exercise, but it can also help to practice it when you're feeling particularly stressed or anxious. Experts believe that practicing mindful breathing on a regular basis can help you do better in difficult situations.

Sometimes, especially when trying to calm yourself down in a stressful situation, it can help to start with an exaggerated breath: a deep inhale through your nose for 3 seconds, hold your breath for at least 2 seconds, and do a long exhale via your mouth. Otherwise, simply observe each breath without attempting to adjust it; it may be helpful to concentrate on the rise and fall of your chest or the sensation through your nostril. As you do so, you may notice that your mind wanders, distracted by thoughts or physical sensations. That is okay. Simply acknowledge that this is happening and gently redirect your attention back to your breath.

Find a relaxed and comfortable position
You could be sitting in a chair or on the floor with a cushion. Keep your back straight but not too tight, and your hands rest wherever they are most comfortable. Place your tongue on the roof of your mouth or wherever it feels most comfortable.

Consider and relax your body
Try to notice your body's shape and weight. Allow yourself to relax and become curious about your body while seated here, the sensations it feels, the touch, and the connection with the floor or chair. Relax any areas that are tight or tense. Just breathe.

Pay attention to how you are breathing
Feel the natural flow of breath in and out, there's no need to do anything to catch your breath. Not long or short, just natural. Consider where you feel your breath in your entire body. It might be in your tummy. It may be in your

chest, throat, or nostrils. See if you can feel the sensations of breathing one at a time. When one breathing cycle ends, the next one begins.

Be kind to your wandering thoughts
As you do this, you may notice that your thoughts begin to wander. You might find yourself thinking of other things, it is not a problem if this happens, and it is very natural. Simply notice that your mind has wandered. Say "thinking" or "wandering" in your head slowly. Then calmly redirect your attention back to your breathing.

Stay here for 6–8 minutes
Observe your breath in silence. You will occasionally become lost in thought, only to return to your breath. Check-in before you check out.

After a few minutes, notice your entire body, seated here. Allow yourself to relax even more deeply, and then express your gratitude for doing this practice today.

You may notice that your mind wanders, distracted by thoughts or physical sensations. That is okay. Simply acknowledge that this is happening and gently redirect your attention back to your breath.

It's important to remember that your goal isn't to clear your mind or keep it from wandering. Your goal is to be completely present in the moment, without judgment. Your mind may wander while you work on this, and that's fine! Simply be aware of your thoughts and examine them without putting additional stress or judgment on yourself.

It may appear simple, but keep in mind that it is referred to as mindfulness practice for good reason. It does not come naturally to everyone, and it is completely normal to struggle with it at first. To improve, as with any muscle, intentional practice is required—and the effort is well worth it.

Chapter 6

Establishing a Support System

An OCD support system is your support system for the duration of your OCD treatment. These are the people you can call at 5 a.m. if you're having a panic attack over the possibility of stabbing your younger sibling while your parents are away on a business trip. Most importantly, they will provide you with helpful support.

According to researchers, people with a healthy support system are more likely to make and maintain progress than those without a healthy support system or no support system at all. The tricky part about creating an OCD support group is that we frequently want to include people who don't fully understand the assignment for a variety of reasons, such as a lack of knowledge, too many stressors, their own mental health issues, and so on.

After years of working in an OCD program where individuals live with other people diagnosed with OCD, I learned that this bond was critical in managing OCD symptoms and maintaining progress in treatment. Some of the relationships formed by these individuals are still in place today and are likely to thrive in the future because they hold each other accountable in a supportive manner. Building an OCD support group can be difficult at first, but only you can decide whether the benefits of freedom from anxiety are worth the effort.

Now that we know it has been scientifically proven that having a good social support system can help people with OCD, it makes sense for everyone to get one, right? I believe so. If you already have a support system, I challenge you to assess your OCD support to ensure that they are supporting you rather than unintentionally supporting your OCD.

One of the most common mistakes people make when building their OCD support network is including people who make them anxious. If they are already anxious, and this person is going to make you even more anxious, whether on purpose or not, they may not be the best option. This happens frequently with family members. Thus, family therapy can be beneficial. For example, if an individual is working on their perfectionism and their guardians are triggered because their core fear is disappointing their guardians, they may not be the best people to support at this time, but they can grow into it.

Another common mistake is choosing support members but never confirming whether or not these individuals agree with their newfound group involvement or that OCD support exists at all. When this occurs, the advantages of OCD support are never realized. This usually happens because asking for help can cause anxiety. It's exposure time!

Individuals frequently make the mistake of failing to communicate how they want to be supported during difficult times with their family members. This is common among people who do not fully understand OCD, and it can result in accidentally feeding the OCD rather than gaining freedom. For example, if your friend expresses concern about inappropriately touching a child, your instinct may be to say something like, "You would never do that because you are a kind person," to make her feel better. However, this is likely unintentionally providing reassurance to the individual while increasing the core fear.

The advantage of using this method is its simplicity, as there are only three steps involved. Anticipatory anxiety may try to convince you otherwise, but keep in mind that all of the situations you're concerned about may not even occur, so you're stressing yourself out for nothing. I challenge you to make the decision to allow yourself to experience uncomfortable feelings of anxiety for a short period of time in order to receive lifelong support.

Steps for Assembling OCD Support.

> ➤ *Identify your members.*
> ➤ *When identifying your members, you should consider a few factors:*
> ➤ *Can you be vulnerable around this person?*
> ➤ *Are you concerned that this person will judge you because of the OCD?*
> ➤ *Will this person help you in a healthy way?*
> ➤ *Would this arrangement cause strain in the relationship?*

Potential challenges

Many people make the mistake of believing that their family members are their primary source of OCD support. However, in some cases, a family member may not be the best option due to situations such as OCD symptoms disrupting the home, causing frustration, OCD symptoms disrupting family members' lives, family members wanting to support but actually feeding the OCD, and so on. It's a perplexing situation because, more often than not, family members want their loved ones with OCD to recover more than anyone else. It is difficult to strike a balance between compassion and frustration;

many families who have a loved one diagnosed with OCD require assistance with this.

Many people with OCD feel ashamed of their behaviors, and this makes it difficult for them to be around family because they feel like a burden all the time and are afraid of being judged for their symptoms. Family members, unintentionally, can be an instant trigger for anxiety due to feelings of shame. While this can be worked out, you will probably still require assistance in the meantime.

Loved ones do not want to see each other in pain. So it's safe to assume that if you're experiencing increased anxiety as a result of a trigger, your loved ones will go to any length to alleviate your suffering. Whether that means coming over with a big tub of frozen yogurt in the middle of the night to make you feel better, lending you a shoulder to cry on, or even performing some of your compulsions for you to relieve stress.

The first two examples are excellent, but a loved one should not engage in compulsions for someone diagnosed with OCD. This is another reason why selecting people who are familiar with OCD and have also undergone OCD treatment can be beneficial. They can relate to how you feel due to the fact they are also going through it and understand how difficult it can be in a way that others cannot, especially if you have similar subtypes or were in identical treatment programs.

Reach out to members
Shame can still have an impact on the effectiveness of OCD treatment if it is triggered by a situation rather than a specific person. This is the shame that prevents us from seeking OCD support, despite the fact that we would likely benefit from it. If this step is not completed, you have done the mental health equivalent of committing to learning to run and then attempting to practice without first lacing up your shoestrings. You need that support to be able to practice and improve.

So, what do I say after I've chosen my team? I can't tell you exactly what to say, but because we know communication is essential, you could take these steps to help you convey your message:

> - *Share your support goals.*
> - *Ask if they want to take part.*
> - *Determine the next steps.*
> - *If they say yes, explain what type of support you require and confirm that they can provide it.*

➤ *If not, respect their wishes and find someone else.*

It's completely normal to feel hesitant. It's difficult to be vulnerable in front of others, even if you're close. However, keep in mind that you are doing this to free yourself from OCD, and ERP has been shown by scientists to be the most effective treatment. If you need more convincing, think about what you've tried before. Has anything you've tried produced the results you desired? If not, it seems like it's time to try something new. Consider what you would do if the roles were reversed and one of the people you chose approached you about something similar. When you're struggling with OCD, reach out to your support system. Whatever you do, remember that your supporters have your back.

Having OCD support will increase your chances of managing your OCD. You build this support by identifying special people with whom you can be vulnerable and receive healthy support. Then contact them, devise a game plan specific to your needs, and put it into action.

Chapter 7

Developing Coping Strategies

Understanding and applying various coping skills is essential for managing OCD. These abilities are typically classified into four categories: emotional, cognitive, social, and physical. Each category is intended to address a different aspect of your OCD experience, and a comprehensive approach that includes all categories can result in more effective management.

Emotional Coping Strategies for OCD

When OCD triggers overwhelming emotions, it is critical to have coping strategies. Emotional coping skills are specifically designed to help people stay grounded and avoid emotional spirals. Here are some proven emotional coping strategies for OCD:

Deep breathing
This technique lowers your heart rate, promotes relaxation, and reduces anxiety. It's a simple but effective way to take control of your emotional state.

Mindfulness
Being present in the moment can help divert your attention away from OCD and reduce anxiety. This entails paying attention to the present moment rather than distracting thoughts.

Emotional Awareness
Recognize and acknowledge your emotions. Don't fight them; just let them be and know they'll pass. This acceptance weakens the power of emotions.

Art therapy
Expressing your emotions through art can help to reduce their intensity and provide a creative outlet for anxiety.

Music Therapy
Listening to or making music can also have a therapeutic effect, helping to relax and distract the mind.

Cognitive Coping Skills for OCD

Because OCD is primarily defined by intrusive thoughts, cognitive coping skills are essential. These techniques are designed to help you gain control of your thought patterns and break the OCD cycle. Let's look at a few cognitive coping skills:

Cognitive behavior therapy (CBT)
This structured therapeutic approach teaches people how to understand and change their thought patterns, which reduces the severity of OCD symptoms.

Mindful observation
This skill entails nonjudgmental observation of your thoughts as they come and go. Detaching yourself from your thoughts reduces their power over you.

Thought stops
This technique entails consciously saying "stop" when unwanted thoughts arise. It is a method of gaining control over your thoughts.

Reframing
This technique requires you to consciously shift your perspective on intrusive thoughts, which helps to reduce their negative impact.

Acceptance and Commitment Therapy (ACT)
This type of therapy teaches you to accept intrusive thoughts without reacting to them, reducing their influence on your behavior.

Social Coping Strategies for OCD

Individuals with OCD may struggle with social interactions at times. However, learning social coping skills can help you manage your social anxiety, reduce feelings of isolation, and provide much-needed support. Here are some useful social coping skills:

Support groups
These groups offer a safe space to share your experiences, learn from others, and feel less isolated in your struggle.

Open communication
Being open about your OCD with trusted friends and family members can help alleviate some of the burdens you may be carrying.

Assertiveness

Learning to express your needs and boundaries clearly can help you build better relationships and reduce stress.

Conflict resolution

Improving your ability to resolve disagreements can result in more positive social interactions and lower anxiety levels.

Physical Coping Strategies for OCD

Physical coping skills are frequently overlooked, but they play an important role in managing OCD symptoms. Regular physical activity can help to alleviate anxiety and improve mood. Below are some physical coping skills for dealing with OCD:

Regular exercise

Physical activity can significantly reduce anxiety and improve mood, making it an important component of a comprehensive OCD management strategy.

Balanced diet

A nutritious diet can boost brain health, reduce anxiety, and improve mood.

Sleep hygiene

Good sleep habits can alleviate anxiety and provide the energy required to deal with OCD.

Yoga

This practice combines physical poses, mindfulness, and deep breathing to effectively reduce anxiety.

How OCD coping strategies work

Individuals with OCD can use coping skills to manage their disorder. They are based on the science of cognitive-behavioral therapy (CBT), mindfulness, and other therapeutic methods, with each aiming to address a specific aspect of OCD.

Simply put, these skills assist individuals in gaining control of their obsessions and compulsions, reducing anxiety, and improving their overall quality of life.

The process of how these skills work can be divided into three stages: recognition, response, and reinforcement.

Identify obsessions and compulsions.
The first step in using coping skills for OCD is recognizing the presence of obsessions and compulsions.

This stage entails distinguishing between normal worries and intrusive, obsessive thinking or compulsive behaviors. It is about becoming aware of your thoughts and behaviors and accepting their irrational and distressing nature.

Using appropriate coping skills.
Once obsessions and compulsions have been discovered, the next step is to respond with appropriate coping strategies. The nature of the obsession or compulsion, as well as the individual's personal preferences, will determine the coping strategy used.

For example, someone who is overwhelmed with anxious thoughts may use mindfulness techniques to stay present and avoid becoming consumed by their obsessions. Someone suffering from compulsive behavior, on the other hand, may employ distraction techniques to break the cycle of compulsion.

Practice and reinforce coping skills.
The final stage entails consistently practicing and reinforcing these skills. This stage is critical for the long-term treatment of OCD. Individuals who use and reinforce coping skills on a regular basis can gradually reduce the power of obsessions and compulsions.

This stage may include establishing a regular mindfulness practice, attending a support group on a regular basis, or employing cognitive-behavioral techniques under the supervision of a therapist.

Other Coping Skills

We've compiled a list of OCD coping strategies. Always remember that OCD is not the fault of the person affected; it is a medical condition, just like any other illness, and should be treated as such.

Avoid drugs and alcohol

Drugs on the street and illicit alcohol can temporarily silence obsessive thoughts and alleviate the pain of OCD, but regular substance abuse can quickly escalate. According to a study published in the Journal of Anxiety Disorders, approximately 25% of people seeking OCD treatment also meet the criteria for substance use disorder. People who develop OCD symptoms as children or teenagers frequently turn to drugs and alcohol to cope with their intrusive thoughts and fear, before realizing that their symptoms indicate a treatable mental health disorder.

Follow your OCD treatment plan

Obsessive-compulsive disorder is a chronic illness. If you take prescription medication to treat OCD symptoms, continue to take it as directed, even if your intrusive thoughts appear to go away. Stopping your medication abruptly can cause unpleasant physical side effects such as headaches, insomnia, and nausea, as well as the recurrence of OCD symptoms and increased anxiety. Without first talking to your doctor, never stop taking your medication or adjust the dosage.

Greeting Your OCD

OCD can feel like an uncontrollable force waiting to pounce, similar to the monster that lived under your bed as a child. Instead of treating your OCD as a faceless villain, give it a name and a shape. Perhaps you should call your OCD Bully, or any other name. Whatever name you give it, it will help bring your OCD out of the darkness and into the light, making it easier to recognize its presence. Next, give your OCD a shape; it can range from a purple blob to a cheetah.

Keep an OCD journal

You may have seen people keep food journals to track what they eat every day while on a diet; an OCD journal serves the same purpose. An OCD journal can help you keep track of your triggers, identify new ones, and assess the overall state of your OCD. Keep your OCD journal with you wherever you go, and record what happens after you complete a compulsion.

When you've finished journaling for the day and read through your entries, ask yourself the following questions.

> ➤ *Why did these situations set off my OCD?*
> ➤ *What would have happened if I had not kept my resolutions?*
> ➤ *What proof is there that my fear of "contracting a serious illness and spreading it to everyone I love" would actually come true?*

Begin writing detailed pages about what caused your OCD and anxiety, and why that trigger was more intrusive than accurate. Write down exactly what your obsession was at the time, and instead of seeking reassurance from others or the internet, find it in yourself by writing down why that obsession was invalid.

You can also include affirmations in your journal. For example, if you're having a panic attack because you suddenly believe you've contracted germs. Write something like "I am not that special." I am not going to be one of the millions of people who contract it. The odds are in my favor. It's difficult not to cringe when you write things like that in your journal, but honestly, if you feel a panic attack coming on, you can re-read what you've written in your journal and feel better. Seeing your fears written down on paper makes them feel distant and less frightening. Journaling reduces their power over your thoughts and actions.

Exposure and Response Prevention (ERP)
When you first start ERP, start with a first-level trigger. Once you've confronted your trigger, wait 10 seconds before acting on your compulsion. Gradually increase the amount of time you spend before using your compulsion until you can perform the task or confront the situation without needing it. As you overcome your triggers, you will progress up the OCD ladder.

Refocus your attention
If you are experiencing OCD compulsions or obsessions, or suspect you are about to develop one, try to redirect your attention away from the situation. You can refocus your attention either physically or mentally. If you still feel compelled to complete your obsession after the refocusing period, try repeating the session.

Physically Refocus Your Attention By:

> *Doing jump jacks*
> *Get up and walk around.*
> *Hum a song.*
> *Play with a fidget toy or other small object.*
> *Pet a furry animal, like your cat or dog.*
> *Mentally Refocus Your Attention By:*
> *List everything you see.*
> *Name all the colors you can currently think of.*
> *Spell your name or your friend's names backward.*
> *Say the alphabet backward.*
> *Recite the lyrics from your favorite song.*

While you are working to overcome your OCD, make time to celebrate your accomplishments. Fighting OCD is difficult, so success should be celebrated like any other achievement. Determine your rewards before challenging yourself. For example, you may decide that if you can wait 20 seconds before finishing your compulsion, you will order pizza for dinner! You don't need to have rewards or set expectations for every scenario, as this can increase stress. Perhaps at the end of the week, you could reward yourself for any progress you've made, or if you decide to confront a compulsion head-on, reward yourself right away. You are responsible for striking the appropriate balance.

Keep busy

If you are not actively engaging your brain and body, intrusive thoughts are more likely to enter and occupy brain space. Deliberate planning of activities, such as hobbies, work, home projects, and time with friends and family, can help you stay focused throughout the day. Simply doing other tasks helps to divert your attention away from obsessions and compulsions. You do not need to plan every minute of your day, but a loose schedule of activities can improve your overall quality of life.

Keep Stress at a Minimum

Living with and battling OCD is difficult work, which is exacerbated by stress. Stress has been shown to significantly increase OCD in people, so managing your stress levels is critical. Include stress-relieving activities in your daily schedule. Whether you go for a run, read a book, or watch TV, setting aside an hour each day to de-stress can be extremely beneficial.

Remind yourself of the facts

It is easy to fall into a cycle of self-doubt and blame, but try to break it. If you begin to feel guilty about having OCD, remind yourself that you have a diagnosed medical condition. Would you be angry at your asthmatic friend if he had to stop and use his inhaler? Of course not, so you don't have to feel bad if you act out of the ordinary or cause a minor delay. You have a medical condition and are dealing with it. There is no need for guilt at the end of the story.

Struggling to practice the skills consistently.

It can be difficult to maintain consistency in practicing OCD coping skills, especially during stressful situations. Here are some approaches to overcoming this challenge.

Establish a routine
Having a set routine can help you practice your coping skills more consistently.

Involve the support network
Sharing your goals with supportive friends and family can help keep you motivated.

Use apps or reminders
Technology can help you remember to practice your skills every day.

Fear of not having effective coping skills for OCD

It is natural to be concerned about the efficacy of OCD coping skills, particularly when first starting out. Here's how to deal with this OCD fear:

Maintain realistic expectations
These skills are not a quick fix, but rather part of ongoing management.

Track your progress
Keeping a journal of your observations and improvements will allow you to see the changes over time.

Seek professional help
A mental health professional can reassure and guide you through your concerns and fears.

Difficulty recognizing intrusive thoughts

One of the most difficult aspects of practicing OCD coping skills is acknowledging intrusive thoughts rather than attempting to suppress them. Here's how to navigate this:

Normalize intrusive thoughts
Understand that everyone experiences intrusive thoughts on occasion. OCD is defined by the overemphasis on these thoughts.

Practice mindfulness
Mindfulness exercises can teach you to accept these thoughts without judgment or fear.

Seek professional guidance
Therapists can teach you Cognitive-Behavioral Therapy techniques like Exposure and Response Prevention (ERP) to help you become more comfortable with intrusive thoughts.

Navigating the complexities of OCD is a journey, but with the right coping skills and understanding, it's manageable. Embracing tried-and-true techniques and shedding misconceptions can lead to significant improvements in mental health. If you or someone you know is struggling with OCD, don't hesitate to seek professional help and rely on available resources; your mental health is important.

Conclusion

Obsessive-Compulsive Disorder (OCD) is a mental health condition characterized by intrusive thoughts and repetitive behaviors that can significantly interfere with a person's daily life. Some strategies can help to manage and mitigate its effects. Here are ten ways to overcome OCD and regain control of your life:

Expert Advice for OCD

Consulting a mental health professional who specializes in OCD is an important step toward managing the disorder. Professionals with experience in Cognitive Behavioral Therapy (CBT) and exposure therapy can provide practical tools tailored to your specific needs. Treatment can help you learn strategies for coping with intrusive thoughts and compulsive behaviors. These professionals offer a safe environment in which to discuss your experiences, explore coping mechanisms, and develop a tailored treatment plan for your specific challenges.

Addressing Anxiety-Inducing Situations

Exposure Response Prevention (ERP), a key component of Cognitive Behavioral Therapy, provides a structured approach to addressing OCD triggers. You can rewire your brain's response to anxiety-provoking situations by gradually exposing yourself to them and resisting compulsive behaviors on purpose. Over time, the anxiety associated with your obsessions fades, giving you more control over your reactions. ERP helps you develop resilience and healthier ways of dealing with distressing thoughts and urges.

Challenging negative thoughts

Recognizing and challenging the irrational thoughts that cause compulsions is critical in managing OCD. Reality testing entails critically examining your fears and doubts to distinguish between legitimate concerns and OCD-driven anxieties. By questioning the validity of your thoughts, you can gain a better understanding of potential risks. This process enables you to defuse obsessive thought patterns, lowering anxiety and compulsive behavior.

Breaking down progress into achievable steps.

Facing fears and resisting compulsions can be overwhelming, but setting goals can help make the process easier. Break down your progress into small, manageable steps. Every accomplishment, no matter how minor, is a step forward in managing OCD. Celebrating these accomplishments strengthens your sense of agency and motivates you to pursue larger goals.

Creating a Support System

Sharing your struggles with trusted and closest friends or family members fosters a vital support system for managing OCD. Surrounding yourself with people who offer empathy, encouragement, and nonjudgmental support can help you feel less isolated. Their understanding helps you navigate the difficulties of OCD and reminds you that you are not alone on your journey.

Practice mindfulness and relaxation

Incorporating mindfulness techniques into your daily routine can help reduce anxiety and stress caused by OCD. Deep breathing, meditation, and progressive muscle relaxation all aid in relaxation and emotional regulation. Focusing on the present moment allows you to temporarily detach from obsessive thoughts and create mental space for managing compulsive urges.

Stability through Structured Living

A regular daily routine provides stability and predictability, which are helpful in managing OCD symptoms. Consistency in daily activities can help to reduce uncertainty and anxiety triggers. Prioritizing regular sleep, meals, exercise, and leisure activities establishes a framework that promotes emotional health.

Reducing Compulsive Behaviors Gradually

Instead of attempting to eliminate compulsions abruptly, consider working with your therapist to gradually reduce them. This approach acknowledges the role of compulsions in anxiety management while working to reduce them. Taking small steps toward limiting compulsions can help you make long-term progress and develop healthier coping mechanisms.

Navigating the journey to recovery

Overcoming OCD requires patience and consistent effort. The journey is not linear, and setbacks are inevitable. Celebrate even minor victories; every step forward demonstrates your resilience. Staying committed to your treatment plan and maintaining a positive attitude can lead to gradual and significant improvements in OCD management.

OCD treatment requires time to be effective. Cognitive behavioral therapy can last weeks or months. If you have recently been diagnosed with OCD and are starting medication, it is important to understand that prescription medications are also not immediately effective. It usually takes several weeks of daily medication before consistent improvement is seen.

Unfortunately, this means that you may need to devote weeks to determining whether a specific treatment is effective for you. Invest your time. If one treatment fails, return to your doctor. Another treatment option may provide the relief you seek.

The strategies described here provide useful tools for navigating the challenges that OCD presents. As you embark on this journey, remember that your condition does not define you, but rather your determination to overcome it. You can regain control and live a life free of intrusive thoughts and compulsions with the help of education, therapy, mindfulness, and the unwavering support of those you love.

9 798875 709753